Drawing on his 45 years of experience in the martial arts Tony Higo has extracted the essential elements of combat success, in his 'laws of combat' and demonstrates how these may be extrapolated to govern all success, whether it be in the field of business, sport or personal development.

Analysing his own experiences and the wisdom of the great masters such as Sun Tzu, Yagya Munenori, Myamoto Musashi, Tony has attributed the key essentials of combat and life success to 25 laws which are both relevant and accessible to the modern reader.

Condensing definitions, quotations and accumulated wisdom from generations of writers and philosophers together with his unique insight into how the discipline and knowledge of the warrior may be universally applied in life, Tony has produced an entertaining and thought-provoking introduction to these laws, guaranteed to appeal to both martial artists and non martial artists alike.

By recognising, studying and implementing these laws in your chosen field of endeavour, learn how you too may reap great rewards by drawing on the ancient wisdom of the warrior.

ISBN 978-1-4716-2206-9
90000

9 781471 622069

WARRIOR WISDOM

The 25 Elemental Laws that Govern Success in Combat & Life

D1796396

BY TONY HIGO

WARRIOR WISDOM | The 25 Elemental Laws that Govern Success in Combat & Life | TONY HIGO

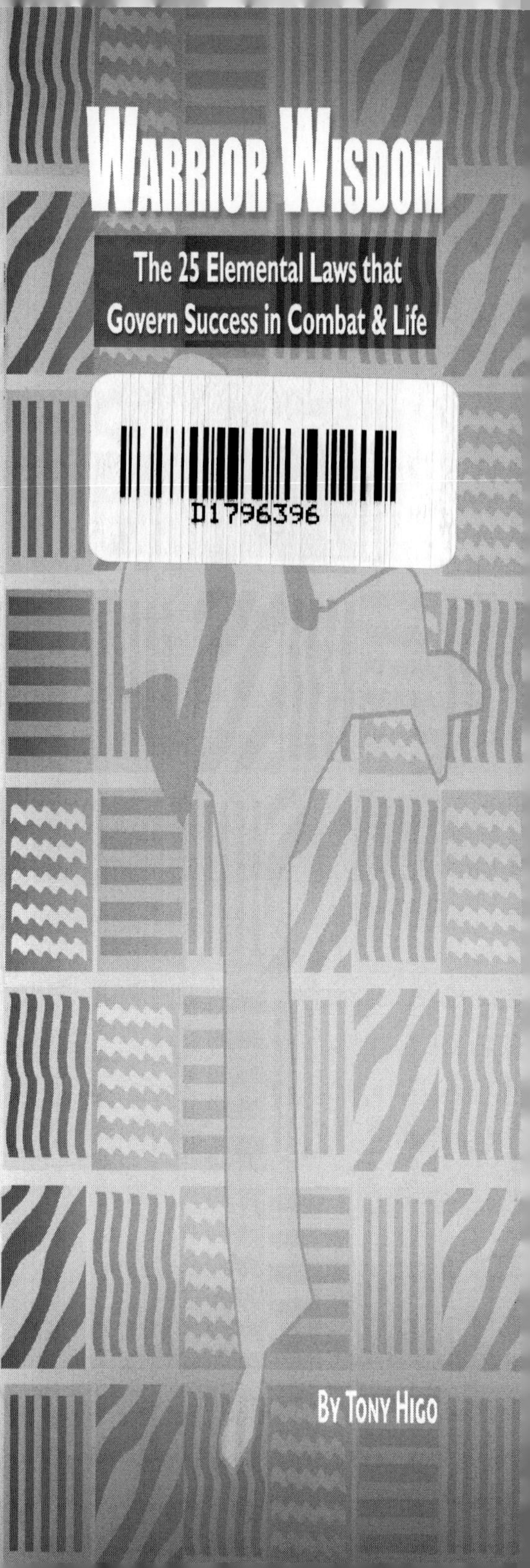

Warrior Wisdom

The 25 Elemental Laws That Govern Success In Combat & Life

Tony Higo

ISBN: 978-1-4716-2206-9

Published by:
Tony Higo

http://www.warrior-wisdom.com
tonyhigo@gmail.com

To My wife Amaya for listening patiently and offering valuable insights and support throughout my writing of this book

Table of Contents

Preface

I have been studying the martial arts for over 45 years and teaching for over 35 and, from my very earliest days, I searched for the 'secrets' of the martial arts; that unbeatable, ultimate technique. This was a naïve search because there is no technique that works every time and gradually, though I wished it could be true, I learned that it could not be. However in my search I did learn that although there is no one 'work every time technique' there are factors that are always present in every technique that works.

Martial artists in general are like I was; they too search for the 'ultimate' technique. When they work together, sharing ideas they share techniques too. They swap them like football cards and add each technique to their 'style' of fighting. But techniques are not enough. They are not the substance of the martial arts, but merely the foot soldiers; the pawns on the chessboard. They are the tools of the chess master, the expendables, but they are not the essence of chess; you cannot win a chess match with pawns, only use them as part of your overall strategy in defences and attacks.

In my search I eventually realised the truth about techniques; that they are the tools of combat much like the tools in the tool bag of a plumber. His toolbox contains many tools of his trade but, although they are valuable and together they are essential, individually they are almost useless. A spanner is useful only on a nut of the same size. Tools, like techniques, are only useful in those circumstances where, like the spanner, they fit. If the plumber does not have the spanner to fit the job he could use an adjustable spanner or one that is slightly too big or perhaps pliers - or if the nut or bolt is loose enough he might even use his fingers. The tool itself, like a technique in martial arts, can be replaced with something else to do the job: neither is essential, only useful.

When I learned this and realised that the acquisition of more techniques, though helpful, like having more tools, could not work in every situation, I then asked the question: what are the essentials of combat, those aspects that cannot be replaced? I began to search elsewhere for my answers.

I studied strategy but, after a while, I realised that strategy, though more useful than technique and deployable in more situations, was not the answer either, because there are many strategies and, though you might blindly use the same strategy in combat, the strategy you use will not always work. Sadly, in the study of martial arts, the teaching of techniques takes a much higher priority than the strategies that lie behind them, despite the fact that strategy is more useful than technique, since it may be employed in more situations. In fact, strategy in martial arts tuition is rarely taught to any depth, whereas technique is taught almost ad nauseum. The strategy of most martial arts schools is founded incorrectly in the number of techniques that the individual combat system offers and the limited number of situations in which they may be employed. This is a subject in itself and not one I intend to pursue here.

Thus I had discovered that the secret of combat lay not in technique, which is very limited, or even in strategy, which though much more useful is still not enough, and so I asked myself again the question: 'what are the absolute essentials of successful combat?' The answer had to be something that lay beneath technique and strategy, something that both strategy and technique relied upon. Techniques rely on strategy but what does strategy rely on? The eventual answer came to me in the form I gradually came to recognise as 'laws'.

Laws are the basis of science, mathematics and even, to a degree, our society. Einstein's work broke new ground in that it challenged conventional wisdom but it also rested upon the work of earlier greats such as Newton. Newton's contribution to science came in part in his recognition and cataloguing of scientific laws. These laws became the basis of much scientific discovery to come after him and Einstein's work could not have existed without Newton's before him.

I know very little of science, but what I do know and did realise was that martial arts are the utilisation of movement, and movement is subject to the laws of science. So my realisation was that techniques and strategies lay on a stratum of laws that govern them. Once I understood this, I began to search for the substance of these laws. This in itself was a challenge as I had to severely challenge and test what I knew of martial arts. This became a process of re-learning or, more precisely, a process of learning what I already knew. What I mean is that much of my martial arts has been acquired over time and with experience. Much of my experience is based on trial and error, in addition to what I have been taught or have learned over the years. Much of what I have learned is subjective, has become instinctive or conditioned over time and I have had to question what I have taken for granted, in order to identify which parts of it were based on 'law' and which were not.

I began by examining and testing what I knew: this consisted of asking questions about what I know and have taken for granted. For instance, in boxing, which is at the core of my martial arts training, you'll hear coaches shout 'keep your guard up!' and this is something I have always been conscious of in my training. In general I obey this rule. However what does it mean to keep your guard up? Is it a technique? No the guard is a technique but to keep your guard up is a strategy. My questions lead me to defining several useful categories that I could use to define my search for the laws that govern combat. I already had techniques, strategies and laws and, through my search, I added two further categories which are rules of thumb and principles.

A 'rule of thumb' I defined as a strategy that, though it did not work every time, was useful much of the time such as; 'a stitch in time saves nine' or 'a bird in the hand is worth two in the bush'. These old adages contain wisdom that has been acquired over many years; they are useful tips to follow but they don't work every time.

A 'principle' I defined as the beliefs that lay behind the combat. For instance there are numerous types of combat and the mindset that lies behind these types of combat are the principles of that combat type. For instance boxing does not use kicks, elbows and several different types of hand strikes. These techniques do not, therefore, form part of boxing techniques, strategies or rules of thumb.

The principles of boxing are based on the techniques that it does and does not use, therefore some things in boxing will respond like laws in that they work every time but they only work every time within the framework of the rules of boxing. For instance, the target area in boxing does not include anything below the belt and only recognises attacks using the knuckle part of the glove. These are the laws of boxing and work every time in a boxing match but outside of a boxing match they cease to be laws and become the principles, that is; laws that work under restricted circumstances or mind sets.

In my search I now had 5 criteria to work with: techniques, strategies, rules, principles and laws, and the laws were what I was seeking. Getting back to keeping ones guard up, I realised that this was a rule of thumb; useful in many situations but not necessary in all of them. So what is 'keep your guard up?' It's a rule but it is based on what I eventually termed the 'law of guard'. What's the difference? 'Keeping ones guard up' is a strategy applied to a technique which is a useful rule of thumb. It could also be a principle in certain types of combat, such as mutual combat, that is; sport combat where one is faced with an opponent as in boxing, with the understanding that the opponent will use a limited number of techniques permitted by the rules of the game. It makes sense to keep ones guard up when you know that your opponent is in front of you and is intending to hit you.

The law of guard applies globally, in the sense that when you have something that is valuable you should protect it. If you have money and want to keep it you should guard it. That is; keep it safe from those who would take it from you. This is a law because it always applies. The law of guard states that 'attack is the best defence' and I chose this as the definition because to protect oneself may, on the face of it, seem to be a passive endeavour in that you don't go looking for trouble, but it is, in fact, a proactive endeavour. You don't wait until you have been hit before you guard yourself as this would be 'shutting the stable door after the horse has bolted' instead you take pro-action which means that if you have something of value you protect it before someone tries to steal it rather than afterwards. I chose the old adage of 'attack is the best defence' to demonstrate the proactive nature of the guard in combat. The guard is the launch point of attack that is the platform upon which attack rests, therefore, if you attack your opponent properly, you will create a guard in that he will struggle to attack you while you are attacking him.

This is an example of how a law works and, hopefully, you can see how it compares and contrasts with the other four categories of technique, strategy, rule and principle. I hope that, through this, you can get an idea of how I chose what finally became the 'laws of combat'.

During my search for the elemental laws of combat, I discovered that what applies in combat also applies in life. It became obvious that combat was a metaphor for life in many ways, it's just that in combat the techniques and strategies etc., are more easily recognised than in life. It is for this reason that I decided to spread the range of this book beyond the purely combative range of the laws so that martial artists could better understand what makes their combat tick and also help them to apply their skills to their lives as a whole. At the same time, I hope to help those who are not involved directly in martial arts to understand how martial arts might help them run their life on more disciplined terms: to understand also why the most famous leaders in history often came from the ranks of the martial (war) arts. This might have been because they were the ones who had grander dreams than others outwith the ranks of their army but also, more importantly, because their training in warfare had taught them how to apply their skills to succeed in a wider sphere beyond just combat.

I hope that you find this book valuable irrespective of whether you study the martial arts or not. I have found it useful to undergo this search myself and now knowing how, why and where the laws apply, I see them more and more often in my life and martial arts training. My search has taught me much about the martial arts specifically and has also opened up a whole new world of understanding on how I can apply my martial arts toward improving my life as a whole. I hope that you will find them as useful as I have.

What are the Laws of Combat?

The laws of combat are evident in the elemental principles that govern life and war. Life is global and war is specific. It is clear that war employs strategies and techniques but that these same principles are equally valid in everyday life may be less apparent until we take time to examine them more closely.

On the face of it, war seems to involve only violence and killing, but this is not the objective of the wise warrior. He aims to achieve his mission in the knowledge that violence may be unavoidable, and so is prepared for conflict. However, war is costly in terms of resources and human casualties, and so it is always the last resort, when alternative, more economical and less extreme options have been exhausted.

The skills required of a warrior are the same skills that must be applied in order to be successful in any human endeavour. In identifying the parallels and recognizing their significance, we can begin to apply the principles of combat to the enhancement of our life skills.

A person who succeeds in business demonstrates the same attributes as the martial artist who is effective in combat. The difference lies in their respective sources of motivation and perception. The business person may have no interest in the martial arts because he associates them with violence and physical aggression and the martial artist may perceive the business person as being motivated solely by money. Both views arise from ignorance of what the other is about. This is understandable, however they both exhibit the same skill sets and have the potential, therefore, to thrive in each other's arena if they were to apply their respective skills appropriately.

In the world of business the effects of stress and poor diet lead to a lack of physical fitness among its workers, many of whom could benefit enormously from the restorative effects of martial arts training on their health and emotions. On the other hand, many martial artists have nothing to show for their exertions other than a few trophies on the shelf and have not fully appreciated the emotional and spiritual rewards to be gained from their craft. Although both groups employ the same skills to achieve different aims, this may not be obvious to those who have not spent a considerable amount of time studying both martial arts and business management.

This connection has been recognised by many cultures from ancient times to the present and documented in their legacy to us, in works such as 'The Art of War' by Sun Tzu, 'The Prince' by Machiavelli, 'The Life Giving Sword' by Munenori and 'The Book of Five Rings' by Musashi, to name but a few. These philosophers observed the correlation between life success and fighting skills - and they were by no means the first to do so!

Today we seem to have lost touch with this wealth of accumulated wisdom, and the respective fields of martial arts and business seem to suffer for it; the former focused on competitions and the latter on money. Obviously this is a generalisation but the point is that there is much to be gained by rediscovering the knowledge of the ancients and applying it to enrich our lives today in both these and many other arenas of our lives.

My motivation in compiling this book is two-fold. My primary intention was to complement the physical training of martial arts students with instruction on how to be healthier and stronger, emotionally, physically and spiritually. When my martial arts students are introduced to the concept that the skills they are acquiring may be applied universally in every domain, they can begin to actively observe the similarities and use them to better equip themselves for life instead of just combat.

As the course of the book developed, I became aware of its potential to reach a wider audience; those willing and wanting to learn how to become self-reliant achievers in any field of endeavour who might in turn help and encourage others to do the same through a deeper understanding of what governs success globally instead of what may seem to govern success on a more local level.

War is, on the face of it, destructive but from its strategies we can learn valuable life lessons, universal principles, or laws, the knowledge of which can help us all to thrive in whatever arena we make our attempt. All we have to do is study and apply these laws, be prepared to fail and start again and, through this learning process, gain a deeper understanding of who we truly are and our purpose in life.

Study these laws well!

Author's note: in order to maintain the flow of the text and avoid the repetitive use of 'he/she', the pronoun 'he' is used to describe the Wise Warrior, but, of course, it may refer equally to 'she'.

The AEGIS Laws

I have identified the five elemental laws of success in combat as:

ATTITUDE

EXPECTATION

GAME PLAN

IMPLEMENTATION

STUDY

The initial letters of which form the acrostic AEGIS. In Ancient Greek mythology, the *aegis* was a shield or breastplate of legendary power, worn in battle by Zeus or Athena. The five primary laws of AEGIS apply equally to combat and to life, and are the laws upon which all the others stand:

ATTITUDE is the quality which has defined every great achiever in their chosen field. Attitude has many synonyms, but no antonym; no opposite meaning exists. However, you may have the right attitude or the wrong attitude. In order to be successful, the correct attitude must be adopted and sustained throughout the journey to achievement.

EXPECTATION is the anticipated outcome of any action and has two possible outcomes: success or failure. In order to achieve our goals we must have a stronger expectation of success than failure, because we only ever receive what we confidently expect. Even the strongest ability and the strongest desire to succeed can be weakened by expectation of failure.

GAME PLAN is our strategic plan of action. When we have acquired the correct attitude and set our expectation we must implement our plan for its effective completion by weighing the facts at our disposal. Strategy, or lack of it, can make or break achievement, and its importance will soon be realised in gaining and sustaining success.

IMPLEMENTATION is essential, since 'Nothing happens until something moves'. The point at which we take action, sees the conversion of our plans into physical reality. Many would be achievers have fallen and still do fall prey to the curse of inaction. The road to success is strewn with could be's, would be's and wannabe's .

STUDY describes the review process whereby we make our assessment of the success or failure of our venture. We must consider the experience gained from results of our past actions and be prepared to constantly adjust and re-assess to better define our next goal.

These five fundamental AEGIS laws are the basis for all achievement and open the gateway to delving deeper to discover the sub laws which hold the key to becoming the master of your destiny – a truly wise life warrior.

The sub laws of AEGIS have been grouped under the elemental laws partly for reasons of balance and symmetry and partly as an aid to remembering them, with the aim of compiling a manual that allows the reader to dip into it at any time and any place to gain inspiration.

What Defines a Law?

In my search for the fundamental elements of success in combat (and, equally, life success) I considered a number of criteria to establish what distinguished a law from something that might be useful but, unlike a law, doesn't work every time?

I considered five key variables which govern both martial arts and life skills, namely: techniques, strategies, rules, principles and, ultimately, the elemental laws.

Techniques

These are the foot soldiers, the pawns on the chessboard; techniques are the 'expendables'. There are thousands of them, and they apply very well in certain situations and not at all in others. Unfortunately many people have the erroneous belief that techniques will get the results they want. It's probably the 'quick fix' mentality we have today, acquired through TV, radio and other media. In martial arts, students are always seeking out 'new' techniques, earnestly searching for the ultimate one that works every time. However, techniques, valuable as they are, are only techniques and limited in their application in the way that a spanner may only be used on a nut of the same size. Techniques are restricted to the specific arena where they apply.

Strategies

Strategies are the application of laws, rules, principles and techniques. They are enormously valuable and, even if you have but a few techniques at your disposal, if you have a deep understanding of strategy, you can still achieve outstanding results. Some of the best fighters in history only had a small range of techniques; it was how they applied them that made the difference.

Rules of Thumb

A rule of thumb is not a law because a law works every time; it is, however, a highly useful device to help one learn and teach strategies and techniques. In boxing a standard rule is 'keep your guard up'. It's a rule of thumb because although a high guard is highly desired in most circumstances, a low guard can be used deliberately as a strategy to draw your opponent in to your attack. Rules are generalisations that work most of the time and will see you do the right thing most of the time. However, they don't work every time, so they are not laws.

Principles

These are personal laws; that is, they work for you based on your own moral code of conduct or belief system. For example, if you believe in God then all your actions will be governed by your religious faith. As Stephen Covey puts it in the 'Seven Habits of Highly Effective People', principles are our 'true north'; they guide us and create the reality we work from. They work like laws within the frame of reference provided by ones belief systems that gear ones principles.

Laws

After much time and testing of the key elements of life and combat I arrived at the 'laws' as a description of those elementals of nature that govern success or failure. Those elemental rules that one cannot operate without are the laws we live by, they apply every time, just as the law of gravity dictates that 'what goes up must come down' it is a universal truth that applies everywhere on this planet and this became my benchmark for identifying and testing whether a law was really a law or was just a technique, strategy, rule or principle. When you start to live using the laws, you will soon see how they are so necessary in every successful endeavour you undertake. They will become your friends and guides along the way and they will always be there whether you require them or not!

AEGIS and The Five Elements

In China and Japan, where many of our martial traditions, and particularly the spiritual aspects of martial arts, originate, they identified five elements and, though they differ slightly between China and Japan, there are always five: Earth, Air, Fire, Wood, Water. (Some sources include Metal by replacing Wood or one of the other elements) Reflecting the five elemental laws, I established the AEGIS laws also to be five in number, since they form the basis of the minimum requirements of success and, therefore, correspond to the five basic elements.

Earth and Attitude

I chose Earth to represent the laws of attitude because our attitudes are the basis of all that we do and are therefore like the ground that we stand on. Unless we have solid ground beneath us we cannot walk, run or move in any way efficiently and I chose the colour brown to represent Earth as this is the conceptual colour of earth.

Wood and Expectation

The laws of expectation are represented by the element of Wood because, in the same manner as wood, our expectations are living and growing and, just like wood, our expectations they can wither and die. Without the proper nutrients any tree will wither, lie dormant or even die if it goes long enough without the right food. I chose the colour green to represent wood to demonstrate that wood is alive and our expectations are like the green leaves on a tree; constantly sprouting, growing, dying and sprouting anew.

Air and Game Plan

The element of Air represents inspiration, that moment when the right answer comes to us. Inspire means 'to breathe in' as well as 'to have a great idea'. Sometimes when we are feeling a little depressed and out of sorts we can go for a walk in the countryside and, breathing and moving in the fresh air, we return invigorated. Or, as with the structured exercise of martial arts training; at the end of each session we are calm and relaxed, even exuding a sense of serenity. Breathing and proper breath control is an important tool for changing our thoughts and feelings. I chose light blue as the colour of air to represent the sky which is filled with air and is the source we often look up to when we seek to be inspired.

Fire and Implementation

Fire is in constant motion and so I chose it to represent the laws of implementation, which are about action and physical intelligence. Fire never rests and always has a purpose, which is to burn. We can describe people as 'burning with desire' or as having a fiery temper or we can even describe someone who is very active in mind or body as being 'on fire'. I chose yellow as the colour of Fire for fairly obvious reasons but I could have chosen others too, such as red and orange, but I settled on yellow which is the usual colour of our ultimate fire; that of the sun.

Water and Study

The element of Water was an easy choice as it appears in all the traditionally defined elements. I chose Water to represent the laws of study because they are concerned with studying and learning from our actions. Study leads to the deeper questions about our purpose in life and water is an ideal representation of depth as the saying goes 'still waters run deep' which suggests that there is more to someone than is visible on the surface. I chose blue because it is a universally accepted colour for water and dark blue because it suggests that the water is deep, like when you fly over a coastline and view the sea; the shallow water near the shore becomes a deep blue further out in the open sea.

The Elemental Images

Each elemental image consists of 5 lines on the elemental colour background. I chose 5 bars to match the 5 elemental laws. The bars are placed at different angles for each law, for instance; attitude is the earth element so the bars are horizontal representing the layers of rock one sometimes sees exposed in hills and cliffs. The bars in the wood elemental laws are vertical like trees and so each image gives a simple representation of the element it depicts.

The Definitions

To help readers understand and apply the laws of combat I have included a definition for each. In the definition I have tried to encapsulate the essence of the law with a short and memorable description. Most of the definitions are existing quotes or sayings that I have used either as they were or with slight adaptations. I have also included a section at the back of the book listing each individual law with its definition, for easy reference.

Synonyms and Antonyms

Because we often use different words to mean the same, I have included in each section synonyms, that is; words that mean the same as the word I have used to describe the individual law, and also antonyms to represent the opposite meaning. Sometimes it is easier to understand a concept by understanding what it is not as much as what it is.

Quotations

To help you understand the concepts further and to support the concept of each law, I have also included several quotations from other writers and thinkers which give an interesting and informative view on each law.

I have outlined my thought process in this way so that, as you dip into this book, you can better understand why it is set out in the way that it is and how this set up might help you to more easily remember and thereby understand the 5 elemental laws and gradually the 20 sub laws that support them. My goal is to help you first understand how the laws apply in combat, because that is where I drew them from, and then to apply them to your life. In this way combat becomes a metaphor for life and, as with all metaphors, they provide a succinct image or definition that makes a concept easier to grasp.

Warrior Wisdom

The Laws of Attitude

Earth

The Law of Attitude

Definition: *"It's your Attitude not your Aptitude that determines your Altitude"*

Attitude is at the core of everything we do or don't do. Every action we take is dictated by the attitude we have towards it. Fear, desire, optimism, pessimism, apathy: all these attitudes and more are the governors of our success or failure in every endeavour we undertake.

Attitude is also our physical position - our stance - which also reveals our inner position and standpoint. Every action we take is motivated by our attitude toward the goal we seek to achieve. With the right attitude we can achieve so much, yet without it we can achieve nothing.

The wise warrior knows that he can change, train and shape his attitude. We, too, can regain the attitude we need in those times when our emotions overcome the strength of our commitment to the goals we pursue. Attitude is the basis of all we do with our lives and much of what we call our attitude has been conditioned in us from childhood. The attitudes of our parents, relatives, teachers, role models and friends have consciously or subconsciously shaped the way we think.

These conditioned attitudes can be either useful or damaging and it is important to be able to recognise into which category our attitudes fall. The wise warrior knows he can acquire new attitudes to equip him better to achieve his goals. By taking control of his education and conditioning, he can build positive attitudes that will serve him and work to remove those that won't.

Negative attitudes can be removed and replaced with optimism and positive thinking. By learning from those around us who have the attitudes we wish to emulate we can re-shape our thoughts to serve us well on our journey of excellence.

The wise warrior decides what he wants from life and works to make his attitude fit for every encounter or challenge he may face. The warrior knows that he controls his life rather than allowing life to control him.

Synonyms
Mindset, disposition, stance, posture, manner

Antonyms
No opposite to attitude

"It is our attitude at the beginning of a difficult task which, more than anything else, will affect its successful outcome."

William James

"Two men look out the prison bars; one sees mud and the other stars."

Frederick Langbridge

"Ability is what you're capable of doing. Motivation determines how well you do it."

Lou Holtz

"The mind is like a parachute: it works best when it's open."

Anon

"Gain victory with courage and protect your empire with changes in attitudes."

Sun Tzu

COLOUR : Brown, ELEMENT : Earth IMAGES : Arms Folded

Attitude: In Combat & Life

In Combat

1. The right attitude is essential, and in combat there is only one possible attitude: a winning one.

2. The right attitude at the right time can avoid unnecessary combat which is costly and time-consuming.

3. Both aggressive and passive attitudes can be used to deceive our opponents into underestimating or overestimating their chances in combat.

4. The wise warrior guards his attitude and refuses to let others change the attitude he knows he must have to succeed.

5. The wise warrior knows that his attitude is revealed in every physical movement he makes and learns to control his body to only reveal what he wishes to reveal.

In Life

1. Our attitude is the basis of all our actions.

2. Our attitude can be changed by ourselves and by others, and we must recognise this to maintain the correct attitude.

3. The life warrior only allows positive change to his attitude and deletes negative influences from his life.

4. The wise life warrior avoids negative influences on his life, particularly sensationalist media reporting which depresses his optimism.

5. The wise warrior builds an attitude that serves him to achieve what others will not attempt, to fulfill the destiny that he has chosen for himself.

The Law of Recognition

Recognition

Definition: *You can only respond to opportunity or challenge if you recognise there is one*

Recognition is the sensitivity to see opportunity or challenge; to notice that change is happening as the precursor to taking action to meet that change.

Many people labour under the misapprehension that their life is as good as it can get; that it cannot be changed and that they have no option but to play the cards that they have been dealt. They don't realise or recognise that those who live lives that they envy often started out from very humble beginnings. The wise warrior knows that no matter where they begin they can achieve great things and learn to recognise that within every obstacle there lies an opportunity - if they are perceptive enough to see it.

Every successful person that has ever lived became so by recognising something in themselves: the means to achieve what they desired. Great warlords, heroes, writers, poets, scientists and inventors - each of them had the sensitivity to recognise that they could be more and achieve more.

Every person can have the life they dream of if they are open to recognising the opportunities in front of them. In combat the wise warrior watches for opportunities to attack and for challenges that will arise. He recognises his opponents' strengths and weaknesses and, where no weaknesses are evident, he creates them.

The wise warrior knows that every day there are present all around him the opportunities that he may seize to achieve his goals. The wise warrior knows that nothing can happen unless he is sensitive to what is happening around him.

Synonyms
Acceptance, admission, appreciation, perception, realisation

Antonyms
Ignorance

"Admiration; our polite recognition of another's resemblance to ourselves."

Ambrose Bierce

"Ah, beware of snobbery; it is the unwelcome recognition of one's own past failings."

Cary Grant

"Art is the imposing of a pattern on experience, and our aesthetic enjoyment is recognition of the pattern."

Alfred North Whitehead

"Don't worry when you are not recognised, but strive to be worthy of recognition."

Abraham Lincoln

"You must know how to spot opportunities"

Miyamoto Musashi

COLOUR : Brown, ELEMENT : Earth IMAGES : Shaking Hands

Recognition: In Combat & Life

In Combat

1.   In combat look for opportunities to attack and defeat your opponent.

2.   Observe your opponent and look to recognise where he is strong or weak.

3.   Cover your movements so that your opponent cannot recognise your intentions.

4.   Offer your opponent an opportunity and when he recognises it and acts upon it, turn it into a challenge.

5.   Offer your opponent a challenge and when he recognises it, use it to disguise the real challenge.

In Life

1.   Always look around you to recognise new opportunities.

2.   Whenever you think there are no opportunities, you must realise that you are simply failing to recognise them.

3.   Everyone has opportunities, but recognise that it is how you view the opportunities that makes the difference.

4.   Be open to recognising new challenges and prepare your attitude to deal with them with warrior wisdom.

5.   Be pro-active in facing challenge, safe in the knowledge that you are equipped to meet it and that even if you are not, the experience will have prepared you better for next time.

The Law of Emotion

Definition: *"Emotion is the fuel that drives motion"*

The heart is the seat of our emotional intelligence and governs relationships between ourselves and others. Our emotions include fear, anger, courage, confidence, joy, sadness, power weakness and strength. We must seek to control the balance of these emotions, so that we spend more time feeling serenity than sadness.

Emotion has no thought; only feeling. It is a primitive instinct; our warning light which alerts us to danger and provokes our response to fight or flee. Emotional warriors, who rely heavily on their feelings, fight too readily, reacting rather than thinking about their actions. They are at the mercy of their fear or anger.

Emotion is the enemy of strategy and, thus, may be manipulated as a powerful weapon by the wise strategist. The wise warrior knows that, although his emotions are essential indicators, he must not be ruled by them. On the contrary, the wise warrior strives to make his opponent emotional, so that, provoked to anger or fear, they will act rashly and illogically and fall into the wise warrior's trap.

Alcohol and drugs increase our sensitivity to the power of our emotions. This is why those under the influence of such artificial stimulants are more prone to act impulsively and foolishly, taking unnecessary risks or exposing themselves to ridicule or danger.

The wise warrior enjoys the joyous emotions and rejects negative emotions. The wise warrior knows that true happiness is not to be found in the unpredictable tides of emotions which seek to govern our bodies, but rather through deeper, contemplative intellectual and spiritual study, which strengthens our understanding and control, creating a sense of calm and fulfillment in our lives.

Synonyms
Feelings, sensation, vibes, zeal, gut reaction

Antonyms
Physicality

"The emotions aren't always immediately subject to reason, but they are always immediately subject to action."

William James

"The degree of one's emotions varies inversely with one's knowledge of the facts"

Bertrand Russell

"Control your emotion or it will control you."

Marya Mannes

"Your intellect may be confused, but your emotions will never lie to you."

Roger Ebert

"The sign of intelligent people is their ability to control their emotions by the application of reason."

Marya Mannes

COLOUR : Brown, ELEMENT : Earth IMAGES : Smiling

Emotion: In Combat & Life

In Combat

1. Never show emotion or pain in combat as this will reveal a vulnerability that your opponent can exploit.

2. Only show emotion when it is a bluff designed to lure your opponent into making a mistake.

3. Learn to control your emotion in combat, so that you can use it as a weapon at your disposal when needed.

4. Make your opponent emotional or angry in combat and he will forget his strategy and be at your mercy.

5. The wise warrior uses emotion as a strategy against his opponent and never allows it to be used against himself.

In Life

1. Emotion can weaken us by causing us to react without thought, rather than giving intelligent consideration to our responses.

2. Be the master of your emotions not the servant. The wise warrior acknowledges the messages his emotions send him and then carefully considers what action should be taken, if any.

3. Others may seek to disturb your base with gossip, hearsay and lies. Learn to develop 'rhino' skin and remember that emotions are only transitory.

4. Emotion is not truth. Don't trust your emotions without exercising caution, but use them to your advantage, to spur you on.

5. Learn to master your emotions using deep breathing, good posture, smiling and body-strengthening exercise. By harnessing your emotions you will be able to change them at will when necessary.

The Law of Guard

Guard

Definition: *Attack Is The Best Defence*

The Law of Guard teaches us to protect ourselves and our gains; not to rashly risk that which we have worked hard to build: ourselves; our property; our friends.

The wise warrior guards his body and mind (as in: 'stand guard at the doorway to your mind'). The body must be protected from attack by enemies, including illness, which can attack a body which is not fit and strong. The mind must be strengthened by allowing only positive and helpful ideas to enter it, and avoiding negative influences from those concepts or people which seek to attack or pour scorn on one's ideas or accomplishments.

In combat, the wise warrior protects himself by keeping his guard in the best position to both defend and attack. In life, keeping guard means protecting one's home, business, investment and family against physical or financial attack. There are people who would steal your property, and so you must protect yourself with insurance cover. You protect your family from hardship in the event of your death by purchasing life assurance.

We put locks on our doors to protect our homes and savings in our bank accounts to protect against financial distress. We invest our money to provide us with income when we are too old to work.

These measures demonstrate our application of the Law of Guard: wise warriors know how to guard themselves in both combat and life.

Synonyms
Cover, defend, escort, save, shelter, keep an eye on

Antonyms
Disregard, forget, ignore, neglect

"Ask others about themselves, at the same time, be on guard not to talk too much about yourself."

Mortimer Adler

"Fortitude is the guard and support of the other virtues"

John Locke

"God grants liberty only to those who love it, and are always ready to guard and defend it."

Daniel Webster

"Good actions are a guard against the blows of adversity."

Abu Bakr

"If it's a slow race, you have to be on your guard. You have to be patient, but I prefer that."

Michael East

COLOUR : Brown, ELEMENT : Earth IMAGES : Boxers Guard

Guard: In Combat & Life

In Combat

1. Be alert to dangers but not in fear of them- keep your guard up.

2. Attack is the best defence and the guard is a means of defence, so the primary function of the guard is to facilitate attack.

3. If you have no guard you allow yourself to become an easy target.

4. Having a good guard means having to block and parry less. Enemies are less likely to attack a well-guarded position.

5. Don't be drawn into dropping your guard, unless it is an integral part of your game plan.

In Life

1. Be on your guard against the negativity and dishonesty of others.

2. Guard your mind by educating yourself constantly in those subjects that you need to improve upon in pursuit of your dreams.

3. Guard yourself against financial loss. Have a plan for building and protecting your assets.

4. Guard your health by staying fit and eating the right foods.

5. The wise life warrior never drops his guard to put himself, loved ones or valuables at risk.

The Law of Focus

Definition: *"What you focus on becomes your reality."*

It is said that 'what you focus on expands', meaning that whatever you concentrate on becomes your reality. Therefore, in order to achieve our goals, we must devote our thoughts and efforts to them completely.

The wise warrior knows that when he focuses his entire being on an objective, that goal becomes his reality. Too often people focus on the unnecessary, the unimportant and the irrelevant. They aim to achieve worthless accomplishments, such as fitting in with the crowd, wearing the right clothes for a particular image or watching the coolest programmes on TV.

The wise warrior knows that everyone has a purpose in life and must, therefore, focus their attention on fulfilling that purpose. The efforts of the wise warrior are concentrated like a drill bit piercing wood or steel; all the energy is focused on one small point and the breakthrough occurs quickly.

The wise warrior is aware of the unimportant distractions which can divert attention from the task, and is equipped to distinguish between the vital and the irrelevant. In combat, the fighter focuses on disabling his opponent by identifying a weak point and concentrating his attack there. The same principle is applied in life, by focusing on the most important goals first.

The wise warrior knows he can only focus effectively on one thing at once, and so dedicates his focus exclusively to achieving his most essential goals first. The wise warrior raises his focus beyond the shallow water, where he can only paddle, to the deep waters where he can immerse himself; fully committed to his goal.

The wise warrior doesn't dabble in inconsequentialities, entertaining the ego and the lazy mind; instead he commits to a life of active participation in society, assisting and instructing others, so that he may look back with satisfaction on a life well lived which has made a lasting contribution to the lives of others. Each generation has a duty to bequeath a legacy to the next, that they in turn might benefit from - *gigantium humeris insidentes* - standing on the shoulders of giants. In successive generations our achievements have been made possible by building on the legacy left to us, and our children's accomplishments can be enhanced by the foundation we, in turn, prepare for them.

Focus your efforts!

Synonyms
Centre, hub, limelight, point of convergence, target

Antonyms
Off centre, out of focus, off target

"You can't depend on your eyes when your imagination is out of focus."

Mark Twain

"I find hope in the darkest of days, and focus on the brightest. I do not judge the universe"

Dalai Lama

"Most people have no idea of the giant capacity we can immediately command when we focus all of our resources on mastering a single area of our lives."

Tony Robbins

"The key to success is to focus our conscious mind on things we desire, not things we fear."

Brian Tracy

"Don't dwell on what went wrong. Instead focus on what to do next. Spend your energies on moving forward toward finding the answer."

Denis Waitley

COLOUR : Brown, ELEMENT : Earth IMAGES : Telescope

Focus: In Combat & Life

In Combat

1. Focus your efforts on the best targets for the best results.

2. You cannot win by focusing 50% of your efforts it must be 100% or nothing.

3. Let nothing distract you from your goals.

4. Do not be faked out or tricked by your enemy and know that his every action is to divert you from your task.

5. Neither be feinted or drawn. Ignore pain, discomfort or other distractions. Focus only on what is most important to achieve victory.

In Life

1. Set valuable goals that help you and others, and then focus like a laser to achieve them.

2. Immerse yourself in your goals and you guarantee their achievement.

3. Do not be distracted by others who would prefer you didn't achieve so that they look better.

4. Look beyond the immediate gratification toward the legacy that you will leave behind.

5. Balance your goals so that the other intelligences are not forsaken in the pursuit of one single aim. Focus on the big picture as well as the detail.

Warrior Wisdom

The Laws of Expectation

Wood

The Law of Expectation

Expectation

Definition: *We don't get what we want, wish or hope for; we only get what we confidently expect*

The Laws of Expectation concern outcomes, goals and the attainment of targets. The elemental symbol of expectation is wood; a living, growing entity, much like our expectations.

Expectations grow if fed the correct nutrients and, conversely, may wither and die if deprived of these nutrients. Essential nutrients for the growth of expectations are hope, optimism, education and a positive attitude. However, expectation may be suffocated by the opposite qualities of despair, pessimism, ignorance and cynicism.

Nothing was ever achieved without the positive expectation that it could be done: Newton, Edison and Einstein all achieved through their intuitive knowledge that what they believed could be achieved.

As we achieve our goals –our expectations – new goals grow beyond them as we discover that we can expect more as we learn to manage our future expectations.

Our old goals are the stepping stones to our future achievements, constantly challenging us to go beyond that which we have achieved in the past.

The wise warrior studies the Laws of Expectation in order to improve the quality of his life and the lives of those he cares about. The wise warrior takes failure in his stride, learning from every experience, and treating setbacks as minor learning curves that become just another step on the path to success.

The wise warrior knows that, no matter how humble our resources are right now, any goal that we can vividly imagine can be ours, if not immediately, then eventually. Often that which we desire to have immediately brings us little fulfillment in the long run. But those goals that we strive for patiently, chipping away at them over time until we get what we desire, bring enormous rewards. Not only because of the satisfaction in the achievement of our expected goal, but through the valuable lessons we learn along the way.

Sometimes our expectations, when we achieve them, reveal to us that they are not what we really want or need, but they are still valuable because they act as signposts on our continuing journey to fulfillment. Often we may not know what we really want, only what we don't want, and that in itself can be enough for us to begin narrowing down the direction we choose for our lives.

Maintaining worthwhile goals, writing them down, setting a time frame for their completion and preparing a realistic game plan gives meaning to our lives; keeps our bodies and minds active and, at the end of our lives, we can reflect upon a life that was worth living. The wise warrior is aware of the valuable knowledge that we can only have what we confidently expect. If you set a goal that you do not truly believe in or passionately desire, then you are unlikely to achieve it. The wise warrior finds his passion, defines his passion and pursues his passion.

Synonyms
Outcome, aim, objective, desire, dream

Antonyms
Surprise, unforeseen, unexpected

"We can have anything we want as long as we want it more than we don't want it."

Esther Hicks

"If you don't know where you're going, any road will take you there."

Chinese Proverb

"Some people dream of achieving great things, whilst others stay awake and achieve them."

Alan Zimmerman

"Do not spoil what you have by desiring what you have not; remember that what you have was once among the things you only hoped for."

Epicurus

"What the mind can conceive and believe, it can achieve."

Napoleon Hill

COLOUR : Dark blue, ELEMENT : Water IMAGES: Finger pointing

Expectation: In Combat & Life

In Combat

1. In combat we set the goal of beating our opponent, without inflicting undue injury.

2. The wise warrior knows when to fight and when to avoid fighting.

3. The wise warrior knows that fighting is the last resort and not the first.

4. The wise warrior knows that martial arts is not about winning, but about getting what you want.

5. The Wise Warrior knows the precise outcome of the confrontation – Disable, Damage, Divert, Delay, Depart.

In Life

1. The wise warrior applies his skills toward his life goals, while respecting others.

2. The life warrior is always working efficiently towards his goals.

3. The life warrior knows that his martial arts skills are just as applicable in life as in combat.

4. The wise warrior sets goals for what he wants.

5. After every goal achievement the life warrior sets new goals. The life warrior never stands still.

The Law of Predictability

Predictability

Definition: *If you keep on doing what you do, you'll keep on getting what you've got*

The second law of expectation is The Law of Predictability which describes the ability to predict the outcome of certain actions or behaviour.

Experience in performing an action will make it predictable in its outcome. We call this experience 'training' and use it to perfect and standardise the result of an action.

We train our kicks and punches to the point that they are predictable, so that every time we perform them we are confident that their result is already known. A 'jab' will be a 'jab' and a 'cross' will be a 'cross'. This knowledge affords us control of our expectations.

We, like all animals, are creatures of habit and most of what we do every day is more through habit than choice. It has been estimated that 85% of what we do today we also did yesterday.

Good habits have arisen through the deliberate use of conditioning, whilst bad habits have usually grown randomly through a lack of discipline and not being mindful of our behaviour.

The combat tactics of 'fake', 'feint', 'set up' and 'draw' are all strategies designed to employ an opponent's predictability, or habits, against him. The wise warrior trains in order to eradicate predictable behaviour that could be used against him, and to reinforce predictable behaviour that favours his strengths and works for him.

By actively practising the observation of outcomes, the wise warrior learns to manipulate his outcomes to his own advantage.

Synonyms
Expectation, conjecture, forecast, anticipation, prophecy

Antonyms
Unexpected, unforeseen

"You can't teach an old dog new tricks."

Anon

"Old habits die hard."

Anon

"A nice blend of prediction and surprise seem to be at the heart of the best art."

Wendy Carlos

"I don't think I have any particular talent for prediction, because when you have three or four elements in hand, you don't have to be a genius to reach certain conclusions."

Antonio Tabucchi

"I've found that luck is quite predictable. If you want more luck, take more chances. Be more active. Show up more often."

Brian Tracy

COLOUR : Light Green, ELEMENT : Wood IMAGES : Crystal ball

Predictability: In Combat & Life

In Combat

1. Fake, feint, draw and set ups are used as techniques to set up attacks.

2. An unpredictable fighter is hard to fight; a predictable fighter is easy to beat.

3. If you train diligently you can predict an increase in your skill.

4. If you study hard you can predict an increase in your knowledge.

5. Learn to observe and predict behaviour and outcomes. With time and practice you will be able to predict outcomes based on your knowledge of previous actions or decisions.

In Life

1. If you set a detailed goal you can predict a favourable outcome. People often repeat their mistakes time and again because they fail to consider and plan their outcomes, so that their results become easy to predict.

2. If you eat too much you can predict an increase in your weight.

3. If you mismanage your money you can predict financial difficulties ahead.

4. If you fail to set goals, you can expect to get what you've already got. Use your accumulated knowledge to confidently set targets you can expect to achieve.

The Law of Assessment

Definition: *Getting the best of any outcome is in the assessment of risk against reward*

The third law of expectation is The Law of Assessment. Assessment is a constant evaluation process; continuously answering the questions: 'yes' or 'no'; 'do' or 'don't', 'act' or 'don't act'.

Assessment is not a studied judgement process like that of strategic action, but rather an instinctive 'felt' awareness that becomes increasingly sharper over time and practice in its use.

Assessment controls our 'fight or flight' mechanism, the biological reaction to challenge or danger, and the other laws rely on its rapid response and feedback in order to determine the appropriate action required.

The wise warrior is skilled in quick evaluation, balancing facts and figures in a heartbeat, to decide on action either towards or away from the challenge.

Assessment differs from judgement in that assessment is a survival response, whereas judgement is a measured and considered response, based more on thriving than surviving.

The wise warrior knows that failing to take action leaves one open to being acted upon. 'Fate' is not the choice of the warrior: the warrior is proactive in making things happen for a reason, assessing every situation towards an ultimate, overall goal.

Those who seek high risk in every situation gradually lose the ability to choose the quality of their life, as they leave themselves exposed, at the mercy of their emotions. Those who seek low risk realise the same outcome at the opposite end of the spectrum. The wise warrior knows that sometimes he will risk much and at other times he should risk not at all. The balance between these two extremes is where the skill of the wise warrior lies.

Synonyms
Evaluation, estimate, calculation, appraisal, gauge

Antonyms
Confuse, mix up

"Self assessment is universal truth."

Anon

"The more laws are enacted and taxes are assessed, the greater the number of lawbreakers and tax evaders."

Lao Tzu

"When you have to make a choice and don't make it, that is, in itself, a choice."

William James

"Choices are the hinges of destiny."

Pythagoras

"It is by repeating the exercises that you arrive at the point of being able to assess the maa (distance)"

Miyamoto Musashi

COLOUR : Green, ELEMENT : Wood IMAGES : Fork in the road

Assessment: In Combat & Life

In Combat

1. Fight or flight?

2. Attack or defend?

3. Move in or move out?

4. Kick or punch?

5. Once a situation has been recognised we need a quick response in order to decide whether it is a challenge or an opportunity. Does it require more of our focus or do we move on? Is it a danger or a benefit?

In Life

1. Can I trust this person or not?

2. Should I stay or should I go?

3. Buy or don't buy?

4. Invest or save?

5. Assessment of whether a situation presents an opportunity or a challenge determines the tipping point between action or inaction toward achieving it or avoiding it. An evaluation based on feelings, born of our experiences, is derived from our survival instinct mechanism. However, sometimes instinct has to be overridden in order to achieve fulfillment; if we always avoid danger we may never achieve anything worthwhile.

The Law of Proximity

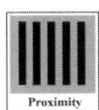

Definition: *The fighter who controls the distance controls the fight*

Proximity is the awareness and control of distance in either time or space. The space between two opponents exists both in geographical distance and chronological time.

The wise warrior understands how best to use distance to his advantage, for instance; the closer he is to his opponent, the higher he keeps his guard because of the greater the risk of injury.

The wise warrior knows that, just as steps will take him closer to his objective in the physical realm, so will seconds in the dimension of time.

Every goal we set is currently getting closer in time. We can do nothing to prevent that, but we can use our time effectively to complete the tasks necessary in the time available.

The wise warrior knows which weapons and tools are effective at any given range and how close he can allow an opponent to approach before they become a threat; a calculation which includes the degree of danger they pose and the armoury of weapons available to them at any given distance.

The wise warrior is aware of his optimum fighting range and aims to keep his opponent in that range, rather than allowing the opponent to select their own comfort zone.

The warrior who best controls the distance to his advantage is the master of the fight. The life warrior who controls the distance between where he is and where he wants to go, is the master of his destiny.

Synonyms
Distance, gap, range, space, maa (Japanese)

Antonyms
No opposite

"The fastest attack uses the closest weapon to the nearest target."

Tony Higo

"Keep him at arm's length."

Anon

"Fill the unforgiving minute with sixty seconds' worth of distance run."

Rudyard Kipling

"One sees qualities at a distance and defects at close range."

Victor Hugo

"The distance between insanity and genius is measured only by success."

Bruce Feirstein

COLOUR : Light Green, ELEMENT : Wood IMAGES : Arms outstretched

Proximity: In Combat & Life

In Combat

1. Be aware of your 5 distances and your 5 levels, so that you can build skill in distancing

2. Stay away from a wrestler so he can't grapple.

3. Put a boxer on his back so he can't punch.

4. Keep close to a kicker so he can't kick.

5. Always stay at the range that is best for you.

In Life

1. The life warrior organises his time and work to utilise the time available to complete the task at hand.

2. Don't be so close to danger that you have insufficient time to react.

3. Make a daily list of everything that needs to be done and how long it will take to do.

4. Every goal is getting closer by the minute.

5. Tempus fugit' –time flies- so don't waste it.

The Law of Balance

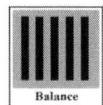

Definition: *Without balance we can never be wholly successful*

With good balance we can achieve almost anything we desire, without it we can achieve nothing that is lasting

Balance is a key law which is fundamental to all the mental and physical laws and influences everything we do.

Balance can be an outcome in itself; creating equilibrium in all areas of heart, mind, body and spirit.

Balance is easily lost and difficult to regain, or even maintain. In order to be sustained, balance demands our diligent attention and awareness.

A mind out of balance is perceived as unstable, dangerous even, and a body out of balance will soon fall.

The wise warrior strives to maintain balance in every aspect of his life, knowing that true success is balanced success.

Success in business at the expense of one's relationships upsets life balance. Likewise successful wealth is meaningless without successful health with which to enjoy it. The annals of history are littered with examples of those who have been outstandingly successful in one field of human endeavour, but woefully lacking in other areas.

Synonyms
Equilibrium, poise, stability, steadfastness, symmetry

Antonyms
Unbalanced, unstable, uneven, asymmetrical

"The best and safest thing is to keep a balance in your life, acknowledging the great powers around us and in us. If you can do that, and live that way, you are really a wise man."

Euripides

"We come into this world head first and go out feet first; in between it is all a matter of balance."

Paul Boese

"The calm and balanced mind is the strong and great mind; the hurried and agitated mind is the weak one."

Wallace D. Wattles

"keep the enemy off balance, even feigning assistance to him"

Sun Tzu

"to practice strategy it is necessary to integrate the whole of ones body without having any imbalances"

Miyamoto Musashi

COLOUR : Light Green, ELEMENT : Wood IMAGES : Tightrope walker

Balance: In Combat & Life

In Combat

1. Fighting requires the constant adjustment of balance.

2. Every step or movement challenges the control of our balance.

3. Every technique we throw or attempt challenges our balance.

4. Speed and power both rely on good balance.

5. Attack and defence rely on mastery of balance.

In Life

1. A life out of balance is heading for disaster.

2. Balance your goals equally with the other four intelligences: heart, mind, body and spirit.

3. Balance thinking with action, action with emotion and emotion with spirit.

4. The achievement of a balanced life is the ultimate outcome of all successful endeavour.

5. Harmony is reached when we have total balance.

Warrior Wisdom
The Laws of Game Plan

Air

The Law of Game Plan

Definition: ***Proper planning prevents poor performance***

The wise warrior makes his move based on his calculations of the outcomes of his proposed actions. It is a well-known fact that 'fools rush in where angels fear to tread', and the wise warrior is no fool.

Game planning is the strategic use of intellect and resources to achieve a desired outcome. Intellect is demonstrated by the posing of appropriate questions and the provision of a selection of relevant answers from which the optimum solution may be ascertained.

The martial arts are simply an emotional response if they are without a measured and considered strategy to convert our desires into tangible and achievable results. Emotion is the enemy of strategy and, therefore, the weapon of the cunning strategist.

Every action we take is strategic, whether or not we are aware of it; everything we do has a purpose, whether it be to obtain pleasure or avoid pain. Some strategies are habitual, without us knowing we are using them, while others, such as martial arts techniques, are consciously incorporated into our routines.

Our aims are achieved by combining techniques we have learned (content) with the strategy of how best to employ them (context).

The wise warrior devises his game plan based on the importance of the goal and is confident in the knowledge that he can attain any outcome he desires as long as he can plan its detailed execution: this is strategy.

Synonyms
Strategy, tactics, preparation, design, scheme, manoeuvring

Antonyms
Unplanned, unprepared, unsystemised, uncrafted

"The best strategy in life is diligence."

Anon

"To win by strategy is no less the role of a general than to win by arms."

Julius Caesar

"We do not understand the strategy until after the campaign is over."

Goethe

"Our strategy is how we cope - how we measure and weigh what is to be said and when, what is to be done and how, and to whom."

Cherrie Moraga

"strategy, inadequately learned is the cause of serious wounds'

Miyamoto Musashi

COLOUR : Sky blue, ELEMENT : Air IMAGES : Breathing in

Game Plan: In Combat & Life

In Combat

1. Strategy is not the number of techniques you have but how you apply the techniques you have.

2. Combat strategy may employ techniques such as fakes, feints, draws and set ups.

3. Study your opponent, test his defence, find where he is strong or weak and then make your game plan to ensure his defeat.

4. No technique is launched in combat without there being a strategy behind it.

5. The wise strategist keeps a cool hand and not a hot head.

In Life

1. Strategy may be less apparent in life, where people often travel through without giving thought to the results of their actions.

2. The wise warrior studies constantly, learning about himself, his surroundings and the strategies at his disposal to make his mark on the world.

3. The wise warrior knows how to apply his martial training in his daily life to his advantage.

4. The wise warrior makes plans balanced against all the intelligences to get the very best from life.

5. The wise warrior knows that a harmonious life is his ultimate aim, and uses his strategy to achieve that goal.

The Law of Judgement

Definition: *Good Judgement comes from Experience, Experience Comes from Bad Judgement*

Good judgement requires careful and unemotional consideration of the available evidence to reach a balanced decision on the best outcome

Judgement is essential to all strategy. It is the weighing of facts, attitudes and opinions to arrive at the best decision possible.

Judgement is the assessment of the best approach to take before executing an action. Sound judgement is considered, balanced and calculated and avoids emotion, which is considered to be the opposite of judgement in that it lacks balance and calculation.

Emotion is vital when weighing up situations by intuition, but it is worthless in its contribution to overall strategy, except where it is invoked in an enemy to cause them to act blindly and irrationally. Emotion serves us in an instinctive, survival sense, whereas judgement enables us to develop and succeed. The lowliest of animals can survive, but the wise warrior employs judgement to plan his strategies in order to thrive –and his ability to do so is a measure of his skills.

Judgement is represented by the image of the scales, balancing the options and weighing up potential outcomes against each other before making the first move, and anticipating the subsequent actions, continuously measuring and re-adjusting as necessary.

It is said that 'good judgement comes from experience and experience comes from bad judgement'. The wise warrior remembers his experiences and applies them to his future situations in order to enhance his judgement-making skills and avoid repeating past errors.

Through time the warrior hones his wisdom by drawing upon his past experience to improve his decision-making. The judgement of the wise warrior is never rash, ill-considered or outside the confines of an overall game plan.

Synonyms

Astuteness, discernment, knowledge, prudence, shrewdness, wisdom

Antonyms

Ignorance, stupidity, imperceptions, misunderstanding

"Judge a man by his questions rather than by his answers."

Voltaire

"The tendency to turn human judgements into divine commands makes religion one of the most dangerous forces in the world."

Georgia Harkness

"Courage is not the absence of fear, but rather the judgement that something else is more important than fear."

Ambrose Redmoon

"Never judge a man's actions until you know his motives."

Wayne Dyer

"It is just as cowardly to judge an absent person as it is wicked to strike a defenceless one. Only the ignorant and narrow-minded gossip, for they speak of persons instead of things."

L.G. Lovasik

COLOUR : Sky blue, ELEMENT : Air IMAGES : Scales

Judgement: In Combat & Life

In Combat

1. Judge what will be gained or lost by fighting.

2. Decide to fight only as the last resort, as every fight saps energy and risks injury.

3. Think beyond each attack to the next to be prepared for the outcome of your action.

4. Judge the best attack; the best technique, target and timing.

5. Never fight for emotional reasons unless pressed to defend yourself to survive. Judgement needs a cool head.

In Life

1. The wisest life warriors think on paper and consider all options.

2. Judge people by their actions rather than their words.

3. Judge your motivation and your target's motivation to get the outcome you expect.

4. Once you set a goal and build your strategy you must decide on the appropriate action to take.

5. Don't Judge emotionally as this will skew your judgement. Judgement, like revenge is a dish best served cold.

The Law of Vulnerability

Definition: *To know your enemies weakness is power, to know your own is wisdom*

The greater the knowledge of our target's vulnerability, the greater the power we have over him

Awareness of vulnerability –his own and that of an enemy- is essential for the wise warrior. The knowledge of one's own weakness is key to building strength in mind and body and the knowledge of another's weakness allows incredible power over them.

The wise warrior always deduces where his enemy is weakest and concentrates the force of his attack on that area.

The understanding of vulnerability enhances the understanding of strength, as these opposite qualities define each other.

In one-on-one combat, the wise warrior uses to his advantage his own strengths and his opponent's weaknesses. Similarly, the life warrior focuses his energy on the most attainable aspects of his goal- on its most susceptible parts.

'What cannot be changed must be endured' – and there is little to be gained from fighting a battle you cannot win- but the wise warrior has the potential to make most goals achievable by discovering and targeting where the goal is most vulnerable to his reach.

Synonyms
Defenceless, exposed, sensitive, thin-skinned, unprotected, weak, wide-open

Antonyms
Closed, guarded, protected, safe, secure

"A chain is only as strong as its weakest link."

Thomas Reid

"Our strength grows out of our weaknesses."

Ralph Waldo Emerson

"There's a basic human weakness inherent in all people which tempts them to want what they can't have and not want what is readily available to them."

M. Kathleen Casey

"Nothing can add more power to your life than concentrating all your energies on a limited set of targets."

Nido Qubien

"An actor is totally vulnerable. His total personality is exposed to critical judgement – his intellect, his bearing, his diction, his whole appearance. In short, his ego."

Alec Guinness

COLOUR : Sky blue, ELEMENT : Air IMAGES : Bullseye

Vulnerability: In Combat & Life

In Combat

1.   Everyone has a weakness, no matter how strong they appear.

2.   The wise warrior knows three things about every opponent:

3.   Most people have the same weaknesses physically and mentally.

4.   How to find an opponent's weakness if it is not obvious.

5.   How to create a weakness if they cannot find it at first.

In Life

1.   A goal may seem invulnerable but, throughout history, the seemingly impossible has been accomplished repeatedly, by discovering or creating the most vulnerable point in a goal in order to achieve it.

2.   In life, weaknesses and strengths may not seem so apparent, but the wise warrior knows that they exist.

3.   The life warrior acknowledges his weakness and turns it into strength. Where he is ignorant, he builds his education and where he is unfit, he builds fitness.

4.   In life, the wise warrior understands that the enemy is just a goal to be achieved and that every enemy is, potentially, an ally.

5.   The life warrior uses education and training (the laws of study and conditioning) to eradicate his vulnerabilities.

The Law of Leverage

Leverage

Definition: *Create More With Less*

Properly applied leverage produces maximal force exerted for minimal energy expended

Leverage is the efficient use of resources to maximize force. A lever is a tool which enables us to lift objects heavier than we could lift without it. Leverage is the augmentation of force, in terms of speed, power and timing.

In combat we align our resources, such as our arms and legs, soldiers or contacts to execute a task more efficiently. Leverage is exemplified by the observations that 'two heads are better than one' and 'many hands make light work'.

In life a wealthy person may use his capital as leverage to open up further sources of income, or a footballer may harness the support of his team-mates to achieve a goal he cannot accomplish alone.

Only a foolish man tries to do everything on his own; working harder and longer hours rather than enlisting assistance, only to burn himself out or become disenchanted.

The wise warrior understands the power of leverage and knows how to use it to achieve results effectively.

Synonyms
Advantage, clout, power, weight, connections

Antonyms
Disadvantage, handicap, hindrance, powerlessness

"As a small businessperson, you have no greater leverage than the truth."

John Greenleaf Whittier

"Give me a lever long enough and a fulcrum on which to place it, and I shall move the world."

Archimedes

"Don't make friends who are comfortable to be with. Make friends who will force you to lever yourself up."

Thomas J. Watson

"Mind is the great lever of all things; human thought is the process by which human ends are ultimately answered."

Daniel Webster

"An important lever for sustained action in tackling poverty and reducing hunger is money."

Gro Harlem Brundtland

COLOUR : Sky blue, ELEMENT : Air IMAGES : Crowbar

Leverage: In Combat & Life

In Combat

1. Fighters understand how to align their feet, knees, hips and shoulders to maximise their body weight.

2. The best fighters create great power through leveraging their body weight.

3. Fast, powerful and skillful techniques are developed through training and practice enabling good fighters to generate force far greater than their bodyweight.

4. The wise warrior utilises not just his own force but the force of others to achieve optimum results.

5. The soldier leverages himself; the general leverages his soldiers.

In Life

1. Using your own energy can only bring limited results and will tire you out more quickly.

2. The life warrior studies hard to understand how to use leverage to get results faster and better.

3. The life warrior strives to build greater leverage in all areas of his life.

4. The life warrior recruits others to his cause to create greater leverage than he can alone.

5. The life warrior recognises he is stronger as part of a team than alone.

The Law of Set Up

Set Up

Definition: *Every Action Sets Up A Following Action*

The wise master is aware of the consequences of his actions and, therefore, makes no move without careful consideration. To 'set up' is to 'prepare', like a farmer prepares the ground before he sows the seeds of his crop. The quality assigned to the set up determines the quality of the outcome; the relation of cause and effect. Every set up procedure brings about a consequent result and the wise warrior prepares his actions while bearing in mind their potential outcomes.

There are two types of set up: intentional and unintentional, i.e. those for which we plan and those for which we don't. The wise warrior sets up considered actions, aware of the possible results and knowing that they may be any of a number of potential outcomes, each of which he anticipates and plans for. The alternative outcomes –the 'Plan B's – must be factored into his preparations.

Some actions are set up by the warrior to become habits; these are the techniques and strategies which define his martial art. They are consciously pre-programmed into the warrior's being so that they are automatically-invoked responses.

The expression 'to chance one's arm', meaning 'to give something a try' implies that the effort is random and unprepared. This is not the preferred approach of the warrior, but may be used under circumstances where there is no alternative. In such a situation the warrior relies on his experience and conditioned habits to attain the best outcome available.

Although 'set up' effectively means 'preparation', the term 'set up' is preferred because it more accurately describes a sequence of physical action, such as a jab setting up a cross or a punch setting up a kick. Set up is not just an isolated strike, but also incorporates the consequent action and outcomes.

Synonyms

Prepare, arrange, establish, make provision for, put together

Antonyms

Conclude, finish, unprepared, disorganised

"A strong, positive self-image is the best possible preparation for success."

Joyce Brothers

"A winning effort begins with preparation."

Joe Gibbs

"Before anything else, preparation is the key to success."

Alexander Graham Bell

"But to me the bottom line is: the more education you can give yourself, and the more preparation you can do, the less chance of failing."

Stuart Pearce

"When the enemy talks of appeasement he may in reality be preparing to attack."

Sun Tzu

COLOUR : Sky blue, ELEMENT : Air IMAGES : Left Jab

Set Up: In Combat & Life

In Combat

1. The wise warrior uses set ups to 'test the water'.

2. The set up is one technique preparing the way for another.

3. The set up is used to prepare a follow up or to elicit a response.

4. The set up reduces the risks associated with direct attacks.

5. Set Ups must blend smoothly giving your adversary less time to react.' (See Law of Priority)

In Life

1. The set up is essential to the successful management of our goals.

2. Set up reduces the task to manageable chunks that make the outcome more achievable.

3. The life warrior sets up good habits and disciplines to support his expectations.

4. Without a planned set up we place ourselves in the hands of chance and the wise warrior is not one to leave anything to chance.

5. Every set up paves the way for the next move.

Warrior Wisdom
The Laws of Implementation

Fire

The Law of Implementation

Definition: *Nothing happens until something moves*

The ancient Taoists (pronounced 'Dowists') understood action to consist of two forms: action and inaction. They called this principle 'wu wei'.

The wise warrior knows that not all activity requires action and that, in certain circumstances, the best action is not to act. The principle of *wu wei* is applied when the warrior understands that both responses – of either action or inaction –are deliberate. Everything that brings about the desired result is caused by our choice of whether or not to take action.

A deliberate action is taken with the intent to achieve a desired outcome. An action that brings about an unwelcome result is 'an accident' –an undesirable outcome!

Many people make plans or have dreams, but the wise warrior knows that, without action on what we want, nothing has moved and, therefore, nothing has happened. Winston Churchill once said 'The best thing to do is the right thing. The second best thing to do is the wrong thing, but the worst thing to do is nothing.' The wise warrior always takes action when it is needed, even if the action he takes is that of 'no action'.

If you set a goal or have a dream, it can only happen when you take action towards its attainment; even if you do the wrong thing, it is better than doing nothing. Every result teaches us something and we learn more from a loss than a win. Failure may bring a sense of pain or loss but, in the longer term, you will look back dispassionately and realise that the experience, the lesson that you learned from the failure, has often been of more value to you than if you had succeeded. There is a saying which goes: 'the life you have right now is the exact life you need right now' which means that you need the experiences you are having today in order to prepare you for the challenges you will face. In order to move forward in life, the wise warrior knows that he must take conscious action, whether he achieves or fails is unimportant, but that he made the attempt is the important thing : 'God loves a trier!'

Synonyms
Achieve, actualize, bring about, carry out, execute, materialise

Antonyms
Cancel, cease, halt, pause, stop

"Life is very short and what we have to do must be done in the now."

Audre Lorde

"Human beings must have action; and they will make it if they cannot find it."

Albert Einstein

"Action speaks louder than words, but not nearly as often."

Mark Twain

"I never worry about action, but only inaction."

Winston Churchill

"to properly defend, the attitude must be that of thorough attack'"

Sun Tzu

COLOUR : Yellow ELEMENT : Fire IMAGES : Running

Implementation: In Combat & Life

In Combat

1. The wise warrior knows that action and non-action are both actions and both have their place in combat.

2. Attack is an action that can be direct or indirect, obvious or deceptive.

3. Attack is the best defence, it gives you the element of surprise and momentum.

4. The most effective attacks in combat are deceptive.

5. Attack is made to gain the outcome the warrior desires which can be to both survive and or thrive. Take action, do not be the victim of your enemies action.

In Life

1. The life warrior makes choices based on his desires and then takes action.

2. Without the necessary action nothing is achieved.

3. If we do not take the action we know is necessary then we put ourselves at the mercy of being acted upon. If we do not take action, action will take us.

4. When we defer our action we should only do so as part of our plan.

5. Action, even the wrong action, brings results that we can learn from if we are open to study the results.

The Law of Priority

Priority

Definition: *Put first things first*

T he wise warrior knows that the best action is efficient action, and efficient action comes through prioritised movement. The practice of martial arts perfects each movement, so that every muscle involved knows exactly when to flex to create the greatest effect; just like a car engine whose cylinders must fire in the right order to propel the car forwards.

An example of prioritised action in combat is the rule that 'the weapon moves first' meaning that, in attack, the first thing to move is the weapon towards the target, and the body follows. If the body were to move first, it would telegraph the movement to one's opponent, allowing him more time to defend and counter-attack.

Priority is also expressed in the advice: 'Don't run before you can walk!', implying that certain tasks always have the same priority or hierarchy over others. In the hierarchy of movement in combat, for instance, the lead hand is closer to the target than the rear hand and, therefore, takes priority; the hand is faster than the foot and so punches have priority over kicks. By understanding prioritised movement, the wise warrior moves faster and with more power, whilst using less energy, and is, therefore, able to fight for longer should the need arise.

Another aspect of priority is that avoiding conflict takes priority over engaging in conflict, since avoidance places less demand on energy and resources. Hence violence is always the last resort of the wise warrior, and never the first.

In life we take action based on our expectations and the strategy we have implemented for achieving our goals; we take the necessary action in the most efficient manner possible by placing each step in the correct order. So often people get their priorities in the wrong order, focusing on inessentials before essentials and, apparently, unable to differentiate between the two. Sometimes people allow their emotions to choose their priorities, instead of applying their mental intelligence. The freedom to do what we want might feel great right now, but, in the long term, we often suffer for it. The wise warrior knows that doing the right thing in the present might cause temporary discomfort but will reap lasting rewards later. The processes of getting fit or losing weight may be painful at first, but the benefits are great and the discomfort is soon replaced by exhilaration at the sense of achievement in one's success.

The law of priority can be summed up in the saying 'never put off until tomorrow, what can be done today'. The wise warrior never takes the easy way because it is easy, he takes the necessary way because it is necessary.

Synonyms
Arrangement, hierarchy, precedence, rank, seniority, superiority

Antonyms
Unimportance, randomness

"Action expresses priorities."

Mohandas Gandhi

"Decide what you want, decide what you are willing to exchange for it. Establish your priorities and go to work."

H.L.Hunt

"Good things happen when you get your priorities straight."

Scott Caan

"In a way, I have simplified my life by setting priorities."

Karen Duffy

"In all planning you make a list and you set priorities."

Alan Lakein

COLOUR : Yellow ELEMENT : Fire IMAGES : Flying kick

Priority: In Combat & Life

In Combat

1. The weapon moves first before anything else to ensure the opponent has the least warning of it and thereby increasing its chances of being effective.

2. Speed takes priority over power; power is wasted if it is too slow to hit the target but a lighter, faster attack can set up a powerful finish.

3. The hand is faster than the foot so use hand strikes more than kicks.

4. The lead hand is faster than the rear because it's closer and should, therefore, be used in priority over the rear hand.

5. The open hand is faster than the closed fist because the closed fist creates tension which slows down the technique.

In Life

1. Don't put off until tomorrow what can be done today.

2. Do what can be done and if it can't be completed move to the next most important task.

3. Don't do what you want to do before you've done what you need to do.

4. Don't work for money; instead have your money work for you.

5. Spend less than you earn and save the difference; focus on necessities before luxuries.

The Law of Timing

Definition: *The Greater Part of Success is in the Timing*

Timing is rhythm, cadence and beat. It is the syncopation of movement and control. Timing requires judgement, and judgement comes through experience. We don't know whether our timing is correct or not until the action has been completed. Everything in life depends on timing. Take your heartbeat, for example; it rises or falls to meet the exact timing necessary for every action you undertake. The beat increases when you prepare for action and slows down while you sleep. It races at the approach of danger, in preparation for 'fight or flight'. Even Nature moves to a rhythm of seasons, months, weeks and days.

The wise warrior knows that, whatever the action or goal, the outcome owes its success to proper timing. The warrior practises daily to perfect his timing; constant repetition heightens the instinctive awareness of rhythm. The effectiveness of speed, power, attack and defence all rely on the control and judgement of timing. Timing is meeting the moment fully prepared, in the same manner as arriving for a business meeting at the appointed hour and with the necessary briefing.

The wise warrior knows that his goal is to strengthen his own rhythm and break that of his opponents. Proper timing results in control. Without control we are like fish out of water, outside our natural element and unable to stamp our authority on our environment. In life, we cooperate with our colleagues by coordinating our timing to work towards our common goal and arriving at its achievement together. The successful warrior synchronises his timing with that of his fellow warriors to reach the optimum outcome. A warrior not in time with his comrades fails to be part of the team and so must strive hard to regain their trust.

We perfect timing through practice, having to endure the experience of 'mis-timing' in order to appreciate being 'on time'. 'On time' is not just hitting the target at the right moment, but also arriving there at the chosen time. The warrior who is always prepared and on time demonstrates respect for himself and his colleagues. The warrior who arrives late and unprepared shows that he has not mastered his timing and is, sadly, an incomplete warrior.

Synonyms
Coordination, beat, rhythm, cadence, regulation

Antonyms
Uncoordinated, untimely, off-beat, unregulated

"All things entail rising and falling timing. You must be able to discern this."

Miyamoto Musashi

"Confidence has a lot to do with interviewing – that, and timing."

Michael Parkinson

"Hitting is timing. Pitching is upsetting timing."

Warren Spahn

"If the timing's right and the gods are with you, something special happens."

Rick Springfield

"Speed is a complex aspect. It includes time of recognising and time of reacting."

Bruce Lee

COLOUR : Yellow   ELEMENT : Fire   IMAGES : Dancing

Timing: In Combat & Life

In Combat

1. The wise warrior practises daily and diligently to achieve mastery of his timing.

2. No matter how well prepared you are, speed, power and strength are all wasted if your timing is poor.

3. Work diligently to build your own rhythm and to break your opponent's rhythm. When his rhythm is broken he is like a fish out of water.

4. Without mastery of your timing, you risk being subject to your opponent's time, and, therefore, subject to his control.

5. Cooperate with your training partners; learning to synchronise your timing is essential to bonding as a team, and being part of a team brings great leverage to your actions.

In Life

1. Strive to manage your time to get the best out of every day. You will not get this day ever again- don't waste it!

2. Judge the best time to take action on your goal. This gets easier with experience.

3. Life warriors who arrive on time are taken seriously by their peers. Those who lack control of time and arrive late or not at all are labelled 'unreliable', are out of time with their peers and risk losing their respect.

4. Make time for the important things such as your health, wealth, family, friends and your spiritual wellbeing; build these rhythms into your daily life

5. Live by the rhythms of your body and nature. Work in cooperation with your natural rhythms; be in tune with your life.

The Law of Launch Point

Definition: *On Your Marks, Get Set, Go!*

In combat, the master warrior knows that the best strategy is useless if launched from a poor position. The position must be selected to derive every advantage available, drawing together the resources of the entire body in order to maximise its effectiveness.

Over time and with practice, this launch point becomes second nature, in the same manner as do timing, distance and balance. In fact, the essence of launch point may be defined as the situation where distance, balance, leverage, timing and acceleration are combined in perfect unison. The inexperience of the novice warrior will be evident in his inability to arrive at the ideal launch point; he will be too close, with his weight on the wrong foot and out of time in his movement causing him to perform poorly.

In life, the launch point is equally important; for example, in preparation for a meeting or in planning a holiday. Taking action of any kind relies on assembling the necessary resources to execute the task most effectively. Even when going for a walk, you must prepare for eventualities in selecting the appropriate clothes to suit the weather and collecting keys, cash, and anything else you might need, before you step out of the door. Launch point may be illustrated by the expressions: 'to get off on the wrong foot' and 'to get out of bed on the wrong side'. Both of these old sayings illustrate the importance of setting off from the best point or one's result will be marred.

The launch point is the law which brings the other laws together, coordinating their combined effect. Launch point is preparation and readiness, but, more precisely than either, it is the exact degree of preparedness necessary for the optimum completion of the action. If your technique is weak but your launch point is strong, you can still achieve great results, however, a weak launch point almost guarantees failure or struggle, even with a strong technique. Launch point requires that your stance, footwork, balance, weight distribution, focus and your whole attitude be completely tuned in to the action you are about to initiate.

The wise warrior works diligently to understand and appreciate the importance of launch point; improving the stability of his stance, the mobility of his footwork, the appropriateness of his guard and the assessment of his timing, combined to bring together the best launch point for his action. Consider the launch point of the sprinter on the blocks ready for the starter's pistol; the better his starting position the better his results. This is the importance of the law of launch point.

In life we must also appreciate the significance of launch point, it is said that our decisions about people and places are made within 7 to 17 seconds and that these decisions once made rarely change. The wise warrior knows this and so greets others with a warm smile and a friendly handshake dressed in the appropriate fashion for the situation and with his work place or home presented at its best. The quality of much of our success is found in the quality and preparation of our launch point. Study this law well as its importance can be easily missed.

Synonyms
Ready, prepared, all set

Antonyms
Unready, unprepared, not set

"Action springs not from thought, but from a readiness for responsibility."
Dietrich Bonhoeffer

"Hold your dog in readiness before you start the hare."
Anon

"Luck is what happens when preparation meets opportunity."
Seneca

"The best preparation for good work tomorrow is good work today."
Elbert Hubbard

"Going into the field means that all preparations are in place".
Sun Tzu

COLOUR : Yellow ELEMENT : Fire IMAGES : Diver on Springboard

Launch Point: In Combat & Life

In Combat

1. Make sure you understand what resources are necessary for the action you are going to take.

2. Every successful action, no matter how small, is preceded by the correct launch point.

3. Never launch from a weak point unless you have no other option.

4. Learn to drop into your launch point quickly before and after every action.

5. Just as you prepare your skills through practice and repetition, you must practise and anticipate your launch point in order to ensure optimum delivery of those skills to have the best chance of success.

In Life

1. The life warrior starts every day, every, action fully prepared.

2. Failing to prepare is preparing to fail.

3. Failing to prepare properly may be interpreted by others as a consequence of being less qualified or of not taking the job seriously.

4. Dress appropriately for meetings, fully prepared and starting on time so that you get things off to a good start. This way colleagues understand that you are taking the events seriously.

5. Greet new people with a smile to get social and business situations off on the right footing.

The Law of Failure

Definition: *If at first you don't succeed, try, try, try again*

Too often people treat life as if it were about winning or losing. Life is not about winning; it's about trying. It's about gaining valuable experience and growing as a person, rather than passing or failing in life, as if it were a series of school tests. Every wise warrior knows that failure is rarely fatal and that success doesn't last forever. The only real failure in life is the failure to try.

In combat and life, we must expect to fail, and, yet, keep trying until we get the result we want. In warfare the goal is not simply to win but to get the result we want; winning or losing are just irrelevant constructs of our egotistical selves.

Wise warriors are not concerned with failure, only with achievement. They know that failures are just obstacles along the way; things we didn't consider or deemed unimportant. However, every time the wise warrior fails, he gets up and starts again, knowing that his so-called 'failure' will be useful in future attempts to achieve.

The wise warrior expects setbacks often but gives little regard to them, thinks past them and continues on. It is said that 'failure is the breakfast of champions' and 'there is no such thing as failure, only feedback': these expressions summarise the attitudes of successful people towards obstacles which lesser mortals would describe as 'failures'.

Therefore, expect failure often. Welcome it, for it will make you strong; consider it to be only practice or experience. Never let failure stop you getting what you want. Every failure brings you one step closer to success.

Wise warriors know that when we fail to achieve a particular goal it is often because we are not yet ready for the outcome; the time may not be right for us to fully learn the lesson or appreciate and use what we have gained. This is apparent when the lottery winner often loses all his money quickly through not having learned how to use money properly and the self-made millionaire loses his money only to gain it all back again within the year. The former has not learned the lessons necessary to deserve and keep his money whereas the latter has failed many times in smaller amounts and this has taught him how to get back to where he was, almost without trying.

The wise warrior knows that the more we are prepared to fail, the more success we will experience.

Synonyms
Breakdown, collapse, defeat, downfall, inadequacy, wreck

Antonyms
Accomplishment, achievement, attainment, success, win

"The only real failure in life is not to be true to the best one knows."

Buddha

"Success consists of going from failure to failure without loss of enthusiasm."

Winston Churchill

"Success is not final, failure is not fatal: it is the courage to continue that counts."

Winston Churchill

"My great concern is not whether you have failed, but whether you are content with your failure."

Abraham Lincoln

"I can accept failure, everyone fails at something. But I can't accept not trying."

Michael Jordan

COLOUR : Yellow ELEMENT : Fire IMAGES : Falling

Failure: In Combat & Life

In Combat

1. Combat is not about winning it's about getting the result you want.

2. The wise warrior takes every knock as simply part of the game.

3. The warrior knows that the fighter who never failed is the fighter who never fought.

4. Just because the warrior doesn't fear failure doesn't mean he seeks it. The wise warrior judges his chances of success and bases his attempts to succeed on having a good chance of doing so.

5. The warrior knows he cannot win every battle and losing a battle doesn't mean losing the war.

In Life

1. The life warrior knows failures are just steps on the journey to success.

2. Failure is viewed by the life warrior as mere practice and not something to get emotional about.

3. The life warrior never beats himself up when he fails; he knows that it is the attempt that counts.

4. The life warrior doesn't invite failure or take undue risks. Instead he takes calculated risks and if he risks in a new area he will institute the 'law of guard' and protect himself from heavy losses.

5. The life warrior doesn't enjoy failure or want failure. It is how he responds to failure that marks him as a truly wise warrior.

Warrior Wisdom
The Laws of Study

Water

The Law of Study

Definition: *The more you know, the easier it is to know more*

The Law of Study is the review and deep contemplation of the results of our actions. Deep thinking requires quiet time to reflect upon what has occurred; to examine how we feel and to take stock of what has or has not been accomplished. We cannot avoid reviewing every action we take - it is built into our psyche - and, at times of high stress, we can find ourselves locked into a type of boomerang thinking, where ours thoughts keep coming back again and again.

The study process is evident in the 'shock' we feel after involvement in or witness to an accident, and the Post-Traumatic Stress Disorder experienced by soldiers exposed to the horrific effects of war. The events are replayed by the mind over and over as the mind studies what happened to make sense and order of the events. The wise warrior understands that every action we take will be studied, just as we relive our waking hours in our dreams at night, as our brain seeks to decode and make sense of the happenings of the day.

The conclusions we draw from the results of our actions form an important part of our study mechanisms. The wise warrior knows that how he views his results must be balanced against his own perceptions and those of other people. If these are not taken into account, he can draw inaccurate conclusions based on his own complexes or ego.

Without taking the time to review and to study our results, we can never progress and educate ourselves to take our achievements to a higher level. Study is our means by which we discover the purpose of our life by meditation on what we really want to achieve.

In martial arts we study our results and motives with the aim of further sharpening our skills. Without proper study of what we want to achieve, martial arts is reduced to simple violence without purpose. In life, too, we must ponder our actions to discover our real direction.

Our initial goals are just stepping stones towards our larger goals but, if we don't contemplate what we have and what we will do, we remain trapped in the thoughtlessness of the 'rat race', indifferent to the advantages of our warrior training.

Deep study will eventually bring us to the point where we connect with our spiritual selves and, thus, with our true direction in life.

The wise warrior makes time to study and educate himself, he is a life-long learner. He studies his art, his life and the knowledge of others and uses what he learns to progress; to become a complete, centered individual and a truly wise warrior.

Synonyms
Analysing, attention, concentration, consideration, contemplation, reading, reflection, research, scrutiny

Antonyms
Ignorant, uneducated, accepting, unthinking, inattentive

"We need quiet time to examine our lives openly and honestly...spending quiet time alone gives your mind an opportunity to renew itself and create order."

Susan Taylor

"Study the past, if you would divine the future."

Confucius

"No trace of slavery ought to mix with the studies of the freeborn man. No study pursued under compulsion remains rooted in the memory"

Plato

"When you are offended at any man's fault, turn to yourself and study your own failings. Then you will forget your anger."

Epictetus

"There are more men ennobled by study than by nature."

Marcus Tullius Cicero

COLOUR : Dark blue ELEMENT : Water IMAGES : Reading

Study: In Combat & Life

In Combat

1. The wise warrior studies his opponent before he attacks.

2. The wise warrior reviews each goal attained, learning from every encounter and applies what he learns in his next goal.

3. We learn more from a loss than a win, however we don't call it loss; we call it experience.

4. Study is the thoughtful practice that brings us mastery of technique.

5. Without study there can be no mastery and without mastery there is no understanding.

In Life

1. The life warrior educates himself constantly. Einstein said 'the knowledge that got you to where you are today is not enough to get you to where you want to be tomorrow'.

2. The life warrior reviews every outcome in a balanced way to glean new understanding from every attempt.

3. The life warrior teaches others to assist them but also to deepen his own knowledge.

4. Without study and review of our actions we are moving blindly and without purpose.

5. Make time for your study, meditate on your goals and look for those nuggets of wisdom that lie within every experience.

The Law of Acceleration

Definition: *The control of speed is the ultimate control of any situation*

Acceleration is the control and management of speed. High speed may be as valuable as low speed; more important is the ability to utilise speed correctly. To know when to move quickly and when not to is the crucial knowledge held by the wise warrior.

In attack, both high speed and low speed are endowed with elements of surprise; the former to catch an opponent off guard and the latter to fool him into believing it is not threatening enough to be taken seriously.

The more we study and practise, the faster we learn and improve, until we reach a tipping point where all skill and knowledge comes easily to us. As we continue to learn, the process accelerates as our bodies are freed from the tension and stress of ignorance and error and relax into deeper knowledge that our bodies seem to understand already. The achievement of goals operates in the same manner; the more we achieve, the faster we achieve more. The problems which at first seemed insurmountable and held us back, through time and experience, no longer seem like problems at all.

Likewise in combat; in the beginning even the simplest action is challenging, but, with time and practice, the moves become second nature and our speed of movement becomes pure reflex, unencumbered by conscious thought.

It is this level of control that the wise warrior seeks and which the Master possesses; the skill of seeing the target and automatically positioning and accelerating to hit it at the optimum speed and distance.

The wise warrior understands that optimum acceleration gives us access to and control of our momentum, compounding our skills and knowledge like folding a sheet of paper in half; each fold doubling to increase our knowledge base and skill level exponentially.

Synonyms

Expedition, hastening, quickening, hurrying

Antonyms

Deceleration, retardation, slowing down

"America is a country that doesn't know where it is going but is determined to set a speed record getting there."

Laurence J. Peter

"Fix your eyes on perfection and you make almost everything speed towards it."

William Ellery Channing

"I am not a speed reader. I am a speed understander."

Isaac Asimov

"I've always found that the speed of the boss is the speed of the team."

Lee Iacocca

"In whatever domain, the movements of a good, accomplished practitioner do not appear fast"

Miyamoto Musashi

COLOUR : Dark blue ELEMENT : Water IMAGES : Gun Firing

Acceleration: In Combat & Life

In Combat

1. The more you practice, the more you will achieve control of your speed. The more you control your speed the more you control the fight.

2. The fighter who is outmatched in speed will soon become pessimistic about his hopes for victory.

3. The fighter who is faster has an advantage over any other strategy an opponent can bring.

4. Think in terms of both high speed and low speed and, importantly, about building momentum, which is the unstoppable speed.

5. It is not important to be either fast or slow only to be fast enough to hit your target.

In Life

1. Practise the important skills until they become automatic reflexes: so that they just happen when you think they should.

2. Accelerate your development through the deep understanding that comes through sustained practice.

3. The more you achieve the faster you will achieve more.

4. Don't pursue speed in your results, speed will build imperceptibly. Remember: Evolution lasts longer than Revolution!

5. Don't focus on speed; focus on doing things well and speed will come naturally.

The Law of Base

Definition: *A tall building needs a deep foundation*

Our base is our launching or starting point, from which we build upwards. Physically we can achieve little without having our 'feet firmly on the ground' and not with our 'head in the clouds'. Every tall building has a deep foundation. The roots of a tree stretch almost as far into the ground as its branches reach into the air.

In martial arts, our base is our stance; how we plant our feet for maximum balance, stability and efficiency of movement or position. Whenever we move we compromise the integrity of our base, so that, on taking a step, our base is weakened as we have only one foot on the floor. We regain our balance when we have both feet back on the ground. In combat we move with care to ensure that we are never very far out of base.

Mentally, our base is the starting point for all that we do. Our base might not be very strong to start with, since we have little experience or knowledge to represent our mental stance. As an infant learns to walk, he is wobbly and uncertain, often falling over, but, with time and practice, his steps become sure footed and strong. In time our experience increases and our knowledge deepens, so that our chances of falling are reduced.

The base of our emotions is in our feelings and ego, and as we learn to master them our base becomes stronger. A person easily angered or upset has a weak base and may be easily toppled. A fighter who can be riled to anger is at the mercy of his opponent as his base is compromised by his emotions.

Our spiritual base becomes stronger the more we consider the effect and motivation of our actions toward our purpose. Deeper contemplation of our life enhances our spiritual base, removing the need to intellectualise and complicate, and allowing us to simplify and moderate.

The wise warrior, in all areas of his life, attends first to his base, establishing a firm footing upon which to build his achievements. Like a mountaineer climbing Everest, he establishes his base camp as his centre of operations from where he starts out on his journey to the summit.

Synonyms
Core, essence, foundation, heart, infrastructure, root

Antonyms
Summit, inessential, periphery

"They have undertaken to build a tower, and spend no more labour on the foundation than would be necessary to build a hut."

Goethe

"An Englishman's home is his castle."

Anon

"All fantasy should have a solid base in reality."

Max Beerbohm

"All love that has not friendship for its base, is like a mansion built upon the sand."

Ella Wheeler Wilcox

"An aware warlord knows that good ground is essential for the mobility of his troops."

Sun Tzu

COLOUR: Dark blue ELEMENT: Water IMAGES: Castle

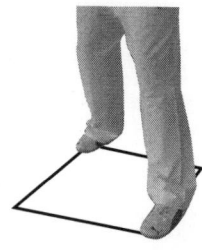

Base: In Combat & Life

In Combat

1. Build a strong yet mobile position from which to launch every attack or defence and you will make every attack more effective.

2. Develop excellent footwork so that even during moments where your base is compromised you can regain your base quickly afterwards.

3. Disturb your opponent's base and you will weaken his physical technique and his mental composure.

4. Disturb your opponent's base and he is weak, as he is unable to develop balance and leverage to defend himself effectively.

5. Disturb his mind and he becomes weaker as his mental equilibrium falters. Take his mind off his goal, confuse his thoughts, and you make him easy prey.

In Life

1. Be a base that others can depend upon, and, in turn, develop those around you so that you may rely on them too. Work on goals that unite you and work together to achieve them. Be a support - a base - for each other.

2. Take calculated risks based on proper planning – you cannot build on your base without challenging its integrity.

3. Don't walk before you can run. Build a secure financial base before risking money on a new venture. Build savings and passive income so that you can look after yourself and provide for your family even if you are no longer around.

4. Build a strong base of health so that you are able to physically complete your goals and enjoy the fruits of your labours.

5. Develop 'rhino' skin so that no one can verbally or emotionally control you. Let your strong mental base be unwavering and immune to negative thoughts or insults.

The Law of Conditioning

Definition: *Repetition is the Mother of all skill*

Conditioning is our self-indoctrination to build good habits and remove bad habits. Much of what we do and how we act and think is governed by habits and conditioning rather than by conscious decision making.

The wise warrior understands that refining a skill requires practice to turn it into a habit. Repetition is the mother of skill, and the wise warrior carefully selects those skills he wishes to build upon and those he wishes to eliminate.

The wise warrior conditions his way of thinking to be positive and optimistic, in order to be helpful and valuable to himself and others. The average person is often unaware of how they are subject to their conditioning, and, as Henry David Thoreau put it, simply live 'lives of quiet desperation'. They seem oblivious to the fact that they can have the life of their dreams by merely changing and reconditioning their thoughts. Not knowing the control they can exert on their lives they become easily conditioned by the media into following fashions and trivial trends that gain them nothing worthwhile.

On deciding which habits to cultivate in all areas of his life, the wise warrior works hard to maintain those habits 'standing guard at the doorway to his mind' in order to defend it against anything that will break his chosen conditioning and divert him from his worthwhile life goals.

We train physically to establish strong bodies and high levels of skill. When we stop practising, our skills and bodies deteriorate, leaving us at risk of falling into easy habits.

Easy habits include eating the wrong food, avoiding exercise, borrowing instead of saving and losing control in our management of money. The wise warrior never seeks the easy life over the disciplined life, and, thus, benefits from a constant feeling of self-worth, progress and achievement.

The wise warrior knows that bad habits are easy to fall into and hard to break. Good habits take time and patience to establish and maintain, but with them come rewards that far out-weigh the effort.

The wise warrior knows that anything worthwhile is hard at first and easy later, like training his martial arts skills; at first they are difficult and frustrating but in time they become second nature and easy to perform. Whereas the unwise pursue easy habits now but they pay later. The effects of habits such as smoking, poor diet and not exercising, may not be felt for years but, eventually, they result in lives becoming marred by ill health and reduced physical capacity.

Work diligently to build good habits, condition yourself to take pleasure in the simple things like good health, an active mind and the wisdom achieved through the pursuit of worthy goals.

Synonyms
Habituate, accustom, programme, train, instill, teach

Antonyms
Out of condition, out of practice, out of shape

"An ounce of practice is worth more than tons of preaching."
Mohandas Gandhi

"Tricks and treachery are the practice of fools that don't have brains enough to be honest."
Benjamin Franklin

"In theory there is no difference between theory and practice. In practice there is."
Yogi Berra

"Practice does not make perfect. Only perfect practice makes perfect."
Vince Lombardi

In ancient days warriors made themselves unbeatable by constant practice
Sun Tzu

COLOUR : Dark blue ELEMENT : Water IMAGES : Push Ups

Conditioning: In Combat & Life

In Combat

1. The saying goes: 'train hard, fight easy'. Build good training habits; always attending first to those areas of greatest need.

2. Build your practice around the heart, mind, body and spirit. Balance your practice thoughtfully, so that no area is neglected.

3. Build effective strategy into your training; the wise warrior knows that combat is as much decided by a fit mind as by a fit body.

4. You never know how long a confrontation will last. Condition your heart and muscles so that your body is strong enough to 'go the distance' whatever the challenge.

5. Condition your mind to always remember that bad habits creep in almost unnoticed. Regularly review your habits to ensure you stay on the right path.

In Life

1. Most people accept the habits they have. The wise warrior knows he can chose new habits that will serve him better.

2. Identify the habits you need to succeed and strive to acquire and maintain them.

3. Expect distractions that attempt to divert you from your chosen habits, and regularly review your progress to check that you are not letting yourself slip back into old, negative ways of thinking.

4. Sometimes those around you will choose to remain in their comfort zone and feel threatened by your progress. Some will even work on breaking your conditioning – stay alert!

5. A worthy life often requires that friends, colleagues and even family are left behind. Your discipline causes you to travel faster than they do. You can always be there to help them, should they need you.

The Law of Spirit

Spirit

Definition: *Live, Love, Learn And Leave A Legacy*

The spirit is our massive intelligence; it is our subconscious or soul. This intelligence thrives on forgiveness, gratitude and contribution. It is our conscience, that little guide inside, that 'rightness' and life guide that keeps us on the straight and narrow.

Spirit is the hardest of all the laws to define, and the most difficult to understand, but, through utilising the other laws, we reveal our true spiritual self. Hard work, high, intense effort, doing things for others rather than for ourselves, being grateful for all that we have, no matter how humble that may be. These actions uncover our spirit, like polishing a rock and discovering the precious gem beneath.

Spirit is our sense of peace, experienced through physical effort and deep consideration of our actions and goals. Those who deny their spirituality, either through rejection of formal religion or through ingratitude for what they have, miss out on the experience that gives our lives purpose.

The true study of the martial arts, which touches and harmonises with all parts of our lives, will show us how to connect with our spiritual selves - that part of us which is truly who we are and which recognises why we are here and the legacy we will leave behind.

Our spiritual intelligence has resources that we can barely begin to imagine, and knowledge beyond our conscious understanding. It contains the solution to every problem we can encounter, if only we know how to connect with it.

The wise warrior focuses on his life, not just for himself, but as a tool to help others recognise and realise their own worth, helping them to follow their own passion and leave their own legacy too. This is the true spirit of the martial arts.

Synonyms

Character, energy, essence, guts, life force, morale, temperament

Antonyms

Cowardice, lack of backbone, lack of will

"My religion consists of a humble admiration of the illimitable superior spirit who reveals himself in the slight details we are able to perceive with our frail and feeble mind."

Albert Einstein

"Humans are amphibians - half spirit and half animal. As spirits they belong to the eternal world, but as animals they inhabit time."

C.S.Lewis

"It isn't until you come to a spiritual understanding of who you are - not necessarily a religious feeling, but deep down, the spirit within - that you can begin to take control."

Oprah Winfrey

"If you want to accomplish the goals of your life, you have to begin with the spirit."

Oprah Winfrey

"Those skilled in the arts of war permit the spirit of the Heavens to flow within and without themselves."

Sun Tzu

COLOUR : Dark blue ELEMENT : Water IMAGES : Meditation

Spirit: In Combat & Life

In Combat

1. The wise warrior carefully considers his outcomes and expectations, and aligns them to a greater purpose than simple vanity.

2. Combat is a tool to be used in developing oneself, and ought not to be wasted on futile, egotistical quarrels.

3. The wise warrior trains diligently and thoughtfully using his martial skills as a way to better understand himself, his life and his world.

4. The wise warrior uses strategy to achieve his aims, so that violence is avoided.

5. The wise warrior never fights a battle unless it cannot be avoided.

In Life

1. We must strive to avoid being drawn into leading an inconsequential life.

2. The spirit is not mean or selfish, nor does it hold grudges nor allow hatred. These are negative qualities of the ego, and the spirit has no ego.

3. The life warrior avoids the trivial pleasure-seeking ways of society and the media, but rather strives to understand the meaning and purpose of his life in order to establish and pursue his destiny.

4. The true measure of spirit is not what we say we will do, but what we actually do and who we do it for.

5. Our true selves are revealed by what we do for others, not by what we do for ourselves.

Summary of Laws

About the Author

Tony Higo, a 7th degree black belt, is the founder of the AEGIS martial arts system and Chief Instructor of the National Martial Arts Colleges based in the UK.

Coming from a long line of illustrious fighters, Tony was first introduced to the martial arts when his father taught him to box in preparation for starting school in 1965.

In a teaching career spanning 35 years, he has trained more than 15,000 students, including British, European and World Champions, and has himself competed on the England team.

In a long and distinguished martial arts career, Tony has studied many martial arts systems, fought in numerous competitions and gained several world records, including entry in the Guinness Book of Records for the fastest recorded high kick record at 10, 25 and 60 seconds and subsequent television appearances. Two of his records still stand, including an incredible 94 kicks in 10 seconds.

Not content to be restricted to one discipline, Tony devised his own multi-discipline approach, based on practicality, accumulating techniques gleaned from elements of boxing, karate, ju-jitsu, wrestling and the finer points of street fighting, to develop his own style - AEGIS - from the Greek meaning 'anything that protects'.

Although a successful competitor and trainer, Tony's real calling is that of mentor and motivator in personal improvement, believing that 'there is no nobility in being superior to another person; the only nobility comes from being better than you were yesterday' (Ralph Waldo Emerson).

Despite being in constant demand as a consultant, author and speaker, Master Higo still manages to indulge his passion for teaching and training his instructors and students each week, while continuing to promote the AEGIS system as a major influence on the international martial arts scene.

Maintaining the family tradition, Tony's wife Amaya, his son Ben, his brother John and two of his sons, and even his great-niece all currently study the martial arts.